GIANT STEPS

GIANT STEPS

FIFTY POETS REFLECT ON
THE FIFTIETH ANNIVERSARY OF THE
APOLLO 11 MOON LANDING
AND BEYOND

EDITED BY
PAUL MUNDEN AND
SHANE STRANGE

RECENT
WORK
PRESS

Giant Steps
Recent Work Press
Canberra, Australia

Copyright © The authors, 2019

ISBN: 9780648553717 (paperback)

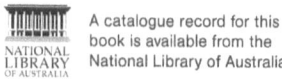
A catalogue record for this book is available from the National Library of Australia

All rights reserved. This book is copyright. Except for private study, research, criticism or reviews as permitted under the Copyright Act, no part of this book may be reproduced, stored in a retrieval system, or transmitted in any form by any means without prior written permission. Enquiries should be addressed to the publisher.

Cover image by Adam Miller, unsplash
Cover design by Recent Work Press
Set by Charlotte Anderson with Recent Work Press

recentworkpress.com

CONTENTS

i
INTRODUCTION
PAUL MUNDEN AND SHANE STRANGE

2
JOHN FOULCHER
BEFORE THE WALK; TWENTY-SEVEN HOURS

4
MELINDA SMITH
MICHAEL COLLINS; 22 NOVEMBER 2018

6
EILEEN CHONG
CHANG'E WATCHES THE LANDING; FIRMAMENT

8
PAUL MILLS
SEASON 1; THE NIGHT HUNTERS

10
PAUL MUNDEN
21 JULY 1969; 16 MAY 1969

12
HELEN MORT
SMALL STEP; JAUNDICE

14
ANNE CALDWELL
TURBULENT SUMMER OF '69 ; ON THE THERAPIST'S COUCH

16
TRICIA DEARBORN
THE EAGLE LANDED; STARFINDER

18
ALEX SKOVRON
WITHIN WITHOUT; AFTERWORLD

20
ROSS DONLON
GIANT STEPS; WALKING ON GREEN CHEESE

22
OLIVER COMINS
MOON LAND; OOOOPS

24
MOIRA EGAN
GHAZAL: MOON; SELENOTROPE

26
DOMINIQUE HECQ
PIERROT LUNAIRE; ALONE WITH THE DARK

28
OZ HARDWICK
ONE SMALL STEP FOR [A] MAN; EARTHRISE

30
ALVIN PANG
WAXING; WANING

32
RENEE PETTITT-SCHIPP
FOOTPRINT; 1 a.m.

34
NESSA O'MAHONY
TRACE; AFTER ILLUMINATION

36
PHILLIP GROSS
MOON, O; SKY SPACE

38
GEOFF PAGE
BUZZ 1; BUZZ 2

40
IAN MCMILLAN
NEIL ARMSTRONG LEAPS; UNCLE CHARLIE'S MOON

42
MARIO PETRUCCI
NONNO; BARRIER

44
PAUL HETHERINGTON
MOON LANDING; MEADOWS

46
CASSANDRA ATHERTON
SPACE COUTURE; ASTRONAUT ICE-CREAM

48
D.W. FENZA
SPACE RACE, 1969; FORBIDDEN PLANET

50
MAGGIE BUTT
THE LITTLE OLD LADIES OF NASA; MAP

52
BELLA LI
INTERIOR OF THE GARDEN I; INTERIOR OF THE GARDEN II

54
LUCY SHEERMAN
NEW YORK, 15 APRIL; CAMBRIDGE, 27 APRIL

56
SAMIA GOUDIE
SEWING THE MOON; A WINTER MOON

58
JILL JONES
LUNAR, NAKED; GIANT STEPS, ATLANTIC RECORDS SD 1311, 1960

60
ANNE CASEY
SINGULARITY; BLESSED AMONGST LUNACIES

62
NILOOFAR FANAIYAN
NOSTALGIA; MOON IN TOKYO

64
KEIJIRO SUGA
WHAT WE DIDN'T KNOW; MOTHER MOON

66
ROBYN BOLAM
SMALL STEPS; UP TO US

68
MARTIN DOLAN
VACUUM PACK ; THE ASTROPHYSICIST TO HIS LOVE

70
RIVER WOLTON
NEIL AND BUZZ TWO-STEP AT TRANQUILITY; FATOUMATA KÉBÉ CLEANS UP

72
CHRISTIAN BÖK
ORCHESTRINO; #DEARMOON

74
JAMES SUTHERLAND-SMITH
MOONDUST; VIOLATION

76
ANDY JACKSON
VIEW FROM THE MOON, 1969; DEAR MOON

78
MATT HETHERINGTON
MAY AS WELL PLAY; SPACE

80
PAUL CLIFF
EAGLE DEBRIEFING: STILL LIFE; SKYFALL

82
SHANE STRANGE
COMMUNION ELEMENTS; CONSPIRACY THEORY

84
BENJAMIN DODDS
CONSPIRACY; CLOSEST I'LL COME

86
OWEN BULLOCK
TOYSCAPE; SEVEN MOON HAIKU

88
LISA GORTON
MOON; SUN AND MOON

90
MAURA DOOLEY
COUNTING BACKWARDS

92
LISA BROCKWELL
O(R)BIT.; STABLE

94
VAHNI CAPILDEO
FOR WHOM THE MOON: I; FOR WHOM THE MOON: II

96
ALISON HAWTHORNE DEMING
NEIL ARMSTRONG'S HEART; DEAR MOON

98
KATHARINE COLES
FLY ME

100
JEN WEBB
EAGLE AT TRANQUILITY; ON THE DARKER SIDE

102
BIOGRAPHIES

INTRODUCTION

'That's one small step for man, one giant leap for mankind.'

On 21 July, 1969, Neil Armstrong spoke these words as he became the first person to step foot on the moon. His utterance defines the historic moment with a twin perspective, connecting his own small physical act with the phenomenal, collaborative scientific program that had conceived of the venture—and made it possible. Some eight years earlier, US President John F. Kennedy had declared, 'I believe that this nation should commit itself to achieving the goal, before this decade is out, of landing a man on the moon and returning him safely to the Earth.' (Kennedy 1961) Those words belie the fact that the goal was also a race against the Soviets; nevertheless, they captured the imagination, just as Armstrong's words would do when the mission was accomplished. We may since have probed further into space, and even photographed a black hole, but for many of us the human element of the Apollo mission still outshines those more recent technological feats; and it was of course done with computers less powerful than the average mobile phone of today.

To mark the fiftieth anniversary of the Apollo 11 moon landing, we asked 50 poets to produce new work, words of their own to reflect upon the achievement—and the new perspective it offered. As the astronauts looked back at planet Earth, and gave us photographs, we gained a new view of our world. The poets commissioned were encouraged to ponder this and write not only a poem addressing the moon landing itself, but an additional poem in which 'space' and 'perspective' might be treated more broadly. We were probing for ruminations either on the state of our small planet, or the greater space into which humankind had taken a small, exploratory, physical step. For both poems, there was full licence to be oblique, tangential or circuitous. And having set a challenge, we did what we considered to be the decent thing, by attempting it ourselves. Each poet's twin contribution is presented here on facing pages—the moon landing poem on the left page, and the 'space' poems on the right.

Various themes emerged, some of them perhaps predictable, but explored with considerable subtlety—and elements of real surprise. The idea of being the *first* leads to various contemplations on childhood steps—and indeed a broader glance at time, just as Stanley Kubrick did so memorably in the opening of *2001: A Space Odyssey*. The visual quality of the broadcast images of the day is of course noted, as are the various situations in which the writers remember the occasion, just as people do with other events of major significance, 'Like the assassination of JFK six years earlier' (p20). (Though of course, while some of us remember 1969 with great clarity, other poets featured here were not even born.) Something about the three-man team and their flag planting leads to an understandable critique—certainly from the perspective of gender as well as the ecological cost of such progress. The 'peaceful' nature of the mission also comes under scrutiny, with casualties of the space race duly acknowledged.

In the second poems, themes are inevitably even more various. Some are playful, even brazenly comic, and some experiment with space on the page, between words. A number are much darker, influenced by current global conditions and a political climate in which we have witnessed human migration on an almost unprecedented scale. If the Earth, right now, is so badly mismanaged, does the Apollo program begin to seem like a quaint and extravagant 'boys own adventure' of the past, or does space exploration remain a strangely urgent quest, one that might yet prove to be of social as well as scientific significance?

SPACE REFUGEE

At this year's Art Biennale in Venice, there is an installation by Halil Altindere (2016) in the main Giardini pavilion featuring Syrian astronaut Muhammed Ahmed Faris, who travelled to the Mir space station in 1987 and subsequently opposed Assad before fleeing to Turkey as a refugee. His reflections lead him to consider outer space as a potential refuge for those who are similarly alienated from their homelands. As Orat Gat writes, reviewing the original installation in Berlin, 'if no country wants them, let's send the world's refugees to Mars'. Faris talks of space as a place 'where there is no tyranny, no injustice ... Space belongs to whoever wants to learn ... whoever [has] the technology.' His idea of building cities in space for refugees may seem far fetched, but so too, in the past, was travelling to the moon. And there are five major treaties in place, including the 'Outer Space Treaty' of 1967, which would seem to protect such a vision. Within the same installation, Nazli Kan, an Air and Space Law specialist, states that, 'according to the Outer Space Treaty no one can own space ... outer space is not subject to any type of claims of sovereignty'.

A more plausible vision of space travel is that of tourism, also referenced in some poems. But is that not, in some ways, a more laughable proposition than that of rehoming refugees?

FUTURA

Our chosen typeface for the titles in this anthology is Futura, created by Paul Renner for the Bauer Type Foundry in 1927, its Bauhaus/Modernist aesthetic still managing to look new to this day. Futura was NASA's choice for the plaque left on the moon—and the official emblem for the whole mission. It was also used the previous year on the poster for *2001: A Space Odyssey*, but was already in use in the US military, and widely adopted as a stamp of authority. For the Apollo mission it had even greater significance. Futura labelling (yes, stickers) rationalised what would otherwise have been a confusing mess of written instructions from a range of manufacturers. As Douglas Thomas writes: 'Without Futura, the command module would have looked like the tangle of electronics in a modern living room.' '[Futura] lent an official look that the astronauts would quickly, even subconsciously, recognize as the authoritative voice of mission control' (Thomas 2018).

It's intriguing to think how the choice of typeface reflects the international, immigrant expertise employed by the 'National Aeronautics and Space Administration' (NASA).

> America owes its space program to German immigrant scientists, meticulously recruited and welcomed as they fled dictatorships and war. Just as the work of German scientists came to represent America's deepest-held values and futuristic hopes, Futura became the vernacular typeface of American commerce and culture. (Thomas 2018)

*

It was somehow crucially important what was first *said* on the moon. Armstrong's words may have been rehearsed, and misspoken, but they instantly resonated around the world, becoming part of our communal consciousness. The words left behind—printed on the plaque, all in capitals—were important too. We might raise an ironic smile that 'Tricky Dicky' Nixon's signature endorses the statement, but that cannot detract from the fundamental message: 'We came in peace for all mankind.'

As Muhammed Ahmed Faris states, 'the free word is stronger than a cannon and bullet and all kinds of tyranny, and [the] honest word will be victorious in the end' (Faris 2019). We feel it is entirely appropriate that poets—guardians of the honest word, and perhaps in that role more valuable today than ever before—should be the ones to take stock of those words uttered and placed on the moon by Armstrong and NASA fifty years ago.

PAUL MUNDEN AND SHANE STRANGE, JULY 2019

WORKS CITED

Altindere, H 2016 *Space Refugee,* multimedia installation at Biennale Arte 2019, Venice

Gat, O 2017 'Halil Altindere's "Space Refugee"', Art-Agenda, 10 February, at https://www.art-agenda.com/features/239785/halil-altindere-s-space-refugee

Kennedy, JF 1961 'Urgent National Needs', speech to a Joint Session of Congress, 25 May, Presidential Files, John F Kennedy Library, Boston, Massachusetts, at https://web.archive.org/web/20090219141758/http://archives.cnn.com/2001/TECH/space/05/25/kennedy.moon/speech.excerpts.pdf

Thomas, D 2018 Futura: 'How One Typeface Landed on the Moon', *Magenta,* at https://magenta.as/how-one-typeface-landed-on-the-moon-dd31ea17d732

HERE MEN FROM THE PLANET EARTH
FIRST SET FOOT UPON THE MOON
JULY 1969, A. D.

WE CAME IN PEACE FOR ALL MANKIND

NEIL A. ARMSTRONG
ASTRONAUT

MICHAEL COLLINS
ASTRONAUT

EDWIN E. ALDRIN, JR.
ASTRONAUT

RICHARD NIXON
PRESIDENT, UNITED STATES OF AMERICA

BEFORE THE WALK

for Neil Armstrong and Buzz Aldrin

First the clean-up
after a meal for men condemned
to the vacuum of fame;

then the business
of cladding their feet
in clumps of shoe,

tunnelling life to the lungs
from a barrel on the back
that weighs less
than its weight
as they lumber about

fixing the hoses, their clothes a mesh
of cooling capillaries. Locking
everything, locking the locks:
*Locks are checked, blue locks are checked,
lock-locks,
red locks,
purge locks . . .*
Last, the brain's jar,
faces bottled in dim gold glass

and fingers turned to rubber
for an easy gathering.
Encased
now, becoming
legend, they glance a final time
at the capsule's galaxy

and Armstrong takes that step
because he is closer to the door.

TWENTY-SEVEN HOURS
for Mike Collins

Twenty-seven hours of singular space,
the men on the moon a new kind
of myth. For twenty-seven hours,
only his breath, and NASA buzzing

in the dark. Each orbit, forty-seven minutes
of unturning black, unspeakable quiet.
He takes up the camera on cue:
There are three billion people watching
the moon. Here on the dark side, me
and God knows what. Then he stretches
his hand, films what he sees of the infinite:
the pitted expanse of his skin, the rise
of his brow, briny depths of his eyes
and the mouth's vast, unweathered crater.
He smiles, says nothing. Turns it off.

MICHAEL COLLINS

Not since Adam has any human known such solitude as Mike Collins is experiencing during this 47 minutes of each lunar revolution when he's behind the Moon with no one to talk to except his tape recorder aboard Columbia.
—Mission Control, Apollo 11 Mission Log, July 21, 1969, 9.44am

Not-landing, too. Not-landing. Somebody had to.
I liked it. Not-landing. For twenty-seven hours. I

loved it. The far side, especially. Everyone I had ever known,
every city, field, tussock, insect. Wiped. Unreachable

behind that great bleached wall. Me, falling past it, in radio silence,
three-quarters of an hour at a time. It changed me.

Not landing, not wanting to land. (The lunar dust
came in with them, anyway, smelling of cordite). They

descended, stamped their stark footprints in, planted
their flag, their cameras. I floated, steering their only lifeboat.

They did their slow work, positioned the solar-wind sail,
the seismograph, the laser reflector. I travelled, witnessing

the humanless infinite, leaving, returning, leaving again, returning.
They ascended, strewing their hammers, their chisels, abandoning

their lonely boots; that plaque. I waited, suspended, exulting,
the craters scrolling, black, white, black, white, grey.

22 NOVEMBER 2018

Go therefore and make disciples of all nations.
Clouds hang over North Sentinel Island.
A man takes a selfie on a boat with another man

leaning on the rail behind him. John Allen Chau on a boat.
How are they to believe in Him of whom
they have never heard? In the wake of the 2004 tsunami

this member of the Sentinelese tribe was photographed
firing arrows at a helicopter. *And how are they to hear*
without someone preaching? The US missionary

wanted to live with the tribe on the remote island. *For necessity*
is laid upon me. Tribespeople killed two Indian fishermen
in 2006 when their boat broke loose and drifted

onto the shore. *Woe to me if I do not preach the gospel!*
Mr Chau offered gifts to the tribesmen, such as a football and fish.
And this gospel of the kingdom will be proclaimed

throughout the whole world as a testimony to all nations,
and then the end will come
                         American missionary killed

by protected tribe was a passionate adventurer and Christian.
The family of John Allen Chau have asked that no-one
be punished for his death. Sentinelese scare off rescuers

trying to remove John Allen Chau's body. Clouds hang
over North Sentinel Island. A dark figure,
photographed from high above, pointing a bow upwards.

---

22 NOVEMBER 2018 is composed of found text from the Bible (English Standard Version—
Matthew, Romans, and Corinthians), and from online news articles (particularly headlines,
photographic captions, and photographic 'alt text')

MELINDA SMITH

CHANG'E WATCHES THE LANDING

*Maybe we are dead
and don't know it*
—'Dor', Nathalie Handal

Glitter of swords approaching—
are these men who visit? Yet

they carry no longbows. There
is only one sun left; it is deep

and cold in the darkness.
The jade hare is bloomed ice.

Two of them: ponderous, tethered.
They leave marks in the dust.

They raise a banner on a spear—
how to tell them there is no conquest

to be had? Luminosity is borrowed,
and beauty fades with closeness.

I want to ask them about the wall
they have built that snakes across

mountains. What keeps you safe
also makes you prisoner. I watch

them closely: they do not see me.
They do not know I exist, but they

have swallowed the elixir I made.
Now their names will be immortal.

Do they know the price?
They will never be able to return.

They will never sleep again without
my song pulsing through their veins.

FIRMAMENT

I notice the ones in pain
shine more than the others.
—'Nights in the Neighbourhood', Linda Gregg

Walking home alone after dinner,
the shadowed streets menace.
There are no stars left in the firmament.

Your hand reaches from the darkness
and closes around my throat—the twisting cat
outlined in air before gravity takes hold.

One foot in front of the other: follow
the ribbon of road. At home, in the top
drawer: a box of matches. Struck sulphur,

incandescent phosphorus—who first said
there is no smoke without fire? You've taken
all my oxygen. There is nothing left to burn.

SEASON 1

one year old
    learning to walk
        holding on   then letting go

to open arms   total applause
the fall that never happened

you grew up young forever   Mom and Dad
saying your name on the phone
                to their Mom and Dad
as if it's already in the papers

your wife lifted the lid on your simmering future
then put it back
your kids sprawled on the rug

between you always something
at work   in the air   SPACE the innocent claim

but dangerous
the bitch-goddess   you knew it   Miss Unspokenof

silk-white   haunting your nights   sharp as a stiletto
that curve making you want to die

years   and the world has changed around you
no longer yours

Earth is the story now   cyclones fires
flood hunger drought   yet you can't care

after that lift-off nothing comes near

so rapid
  so pronounced
     to where you are now

trapped in the blast

THE NIGHT HUNTERS

gory scenes   strong language
minds crushed under brow-ridge

then long chords
a major key   consciousness

finding its way
to weightlessness

             guiding itself

      controlling the phenomena

deep time scuffed by boot-prints

among animal bones
of the de-fleshed

a playful moment
a spear thrown at the moon

           over the M62

between pylons   wild as the moor skyline

and rising   huge   just as they left it

21 JULY 1969

It's there in the early days
of my collection,
cancelled in Southampton,
between British Cathedrals
and the 50th anniversary
of the first flight from England
to Australia.

Another claims earlier
provenance, Port Washington,
making me recall
the interminable vigil,
my schoolboy impatience
in orbit, waiting
for *then* to become *now*.

16 MAY 1969

Turning back a page I find
my mother's handwriting:
*Daddy and I have been
to this island today
and one day you will too.*
I'm struck by the confidence
of those words, but then—

she had watched me learn
to walk—why doubt?
The postcard shows the quay
where I would land
in distant black and white;
no peacocks; no red squirrels
in their rare, safe haven.

SMALL STEP

This is one small step
one lift   and one drop

the known muscles of the leg
one surface to make it stop

one surface   that is not one thing
but atom-loaded numberless

the hot bright distant
planetary rings   the pull of land

we can't explore   like science
everything I do not understand

one step   one small
we are not quite

alone   we play down
the gravity of it all

JAUNDICE

My son in the incubator is a grounded astronaut
blue-lit, a tiny visor covering his eyes.
When I take him out to feed, his scream
pierces the air, cuts this new element, this room
we must breathe in together. I should describe
the air vents in the plastic—round moons—
or the tiles that gleam like cartoon stars
but I am not really there in the Royal Hospital,
                              I write this from the future
where he is six months safe, rolling on good earth.
I am afraid to say what meant the world to me
knowing it's a far-off galaxy to you.
A mother must have written this before
though repetition makes it no less true—
we all want to believe we are the first,
that our words are steady footsteps
that we're going somewhere new.

TURBULENT SUMMER OF '69

As a child, I had a chart of the moon above my bed,
believed its surface to be bathed in water:
Mare Frigoris, Mare Tranquillitatis, Mare Nectaris.
The landing tilted us closer. Our moon was no longer
a goddess firing her chariot across the heavens,
urging her horses—faster, faster; burning up
with love for Endymion dozing amongst his cattle;
his head cradled by their blowsy, uddery warmth.

Apollo 11 had escaped the gravity well of Earth.
Sputnik was forgotten. I remembered Laika, a mongrel
from the Moscow streets. I lay curled in my father's lap,
wide-eyed in the monotone, TV flicker of Armstrong's
footstep. America flexed its muscle like a Greek god,
planted the stars and stripes into all that cosmic rock.

ON THE THERAPIST'S COUCH

I stare back through time
into dark matter,
the space between us.

There's a brandy-soaked marriage,
the scan of a curled foetus with fluid on its spine,
my one, true love: lost on the rim of Blackstone Edge.

Meanwhile, Andromeda spirals towards
a collision with our Milky Way. She's only visible
to the naked eye on moonless nights.

THE EAGLE LANDED

on floor-polishing day

how I loved
the smell of the wax
the polisher's round twin brushes

the way when you tilted its handle back
it took off across the lino

the polisher silent, its long cord stowed
you herded us into the lounge room
compelled us to sit, to watch

I remember the beeps
from the screen, the men
bouncing

I fell
unaccountably hard, succumbed
to space-lust

years later
I watched the first space shuttle rise

after the local radio station
closed for the night
I woke to static

thought the space shuttle's
line to earth
had failed

ran to hammer on your door
telling you
we'd lost connection

STARFINDER

a cardboard wheel
anchored by a split pin
within a cardboard frame

align the date and time
and it shows you
the visible sky

cerulean blue,
first magnitude stars
picked out in gold

you never lay down with it
just held it above you
and craned

for the names you were learning:
Arcturus, Rigel, Bellatrix,
Canopus, Fomalhaut, Antares

I see you walking out into
the long dark backyard
away from the house

you have no friend in,
Starfinder in one hand
torch in the other

feel the magnitude
of your loneliness
you'll have to travel the emotional

equivalent of light years
to get to
where I'm waiting for you

WITHIN WITHOUT

for J.A.W.

My twenty-first birthday party, such as it was,
took place on a regulation Saturday night
in the lounge of our suburban family home,
which mum and dad had considerately vacated
for the event. Maybe twenty friends came,
and of the gifts I received, I can recall,
but still possess, only the slim silver Cross pen
and *Sgt. Pepper's Lonely Hearts Club Band*.
They say we remember exactly where we were
at moments that change our lives.
              From my coming of age,
two memories converge. It was the weekend
I broke up with my first girlfriend. And scarcely
a month later, in the same lounge-room,
I would sit, transported, staring into
our STC 'Durham' TV, to see Neil Armstrong
deliver his celebrated lines from the fuzzy surface
of the Sea of Tranquility.
              I don't think the moon
has much interest in romantic watersheds,
any more than it cared for that small giant leap.
But after half a century, two moments
in a room just weeks apart orbit each other—
in their wake: a pen, a song, a poem, a farewell dance.

AFTERWORLD

To romance of the far future, then, is to attempt
to see the human race in its cosmic setting, and
to mould our hearts to entertain new values.
– Olaf Stapledon, Preface to *Last and First Men*

Our trust had grown stale as suspicion,
Rumours whispered, or thundered,
We lived by the laws of attrition:
We thirsted, suspected, and hungered
After each other—our desires slumbered,
Eclipsed when the moon was faint,
Yet by night they flashed, encumbered
By the lightning-rods of restraint.

We had lost ourselves in our burning
To translate an unreadable book,
For the essence of the soul is yearning
(I quote Rabbi Avraham Kook);
So we quenched our souls, the rumours
We consigned to the dust of our sleeping,
And—lest our desires consume us—
Our translations we kept in our keeping.

And now, as we squint back behind us
To decipher the journey we've taken,
We ask if the future will find us
Too wanting, or too weak to awaken
Those yearnings so softly forsaken;
To rekindle the sparks of our trust
In an afterworld—having mistaken
Our sleeping desires for dust.

GIANT STEPS

Like the assassination of JFK six years earlier,
I remember where I was for the Apollo landing.

Trans Australia Airlines' Booking Hall.
Philip Street, Sydney. A screen flickers silent pics
above ticket clerks, baggage handlers and travellers.
Pedestrians come and go with lunchtime sandwiches.

Fifty years on and without being too droll,
I posit we all were making hazardous journeys
through space that day. Work. Home in peak. The Relationship.
One small step. One giant step. All in one day.

More crowded than usual on ground floor TAA
the show might have been a glance at other aliens—
the Royals, a Grand Final parade, The Beatles.
The screen shone like a tiny, bright god on a pole.

Already leached of all but subtle colours,
the moon turned black & white then ghost grey.
Two blobs with quivering aqualungs bobbed about
inside a moonscape tank. Boys in Space.

Next, a tiny, tinfoil Stars and Stripes stood
at petty attention while America saluted.
A more pathetic act I never saw.
Question of scale—maybe more.

Later, Armstrong and Aldrin slow-hopped away
from no moon monsters. Golf on the moon.
The flag blew away when they blasted off,
leaving us with a mess of memory worms.

But Kennedy. That hurt, being human.
Brave flash of Jackie's pink dress on the black Caddy.
Death will do that. Oswald. Ruby. Loss of hope
before an abyss deeper than outer space.

WALKING ON GREEN CHEESE

Art begat Science.
Long before, July 20, 1969
rockets had stuck pencil noses
into the Moon, thereby rendering Apollo unnecessary.

Movies, writing, cartoon and comic-assisted blast-offs
had already provided moonscape, moon creatures,
facts regarding moon's curious geology.
Once you believe in the launching pad you're there.

In a typical expedition in 1958, cartoonists Hanna & Barbera,
had Tom and Jerry locate two of the moon's inhabitants—
tiny cat Claire de Lune and myopic, bigger-than-an elephant Moon Mouse—
and complete the necessary geological research. Innocent
as innocence.

In the Final 78 rpm Long Playing report, packaged by MGM,
and released immediately to the public,
Jerry Mouse proved conclusively that the moon is not made of green cheese,
despite appearances to the contrary.
Using empirical research—he bit it, nearly breaking a tooth—
long-standing questions regarding the moon's geology were resolved.

But Science trundled on. Armstrong and Aldrin
bounced about like balloon animals, taking pics
of moon and each other and inventing mantras.
In the meantime, others bent their minds towards further reaches
of space and threats to eternity in a galaxy far, far away.

*Tom and Jerry is an American slapstick cartoon comedy. Its original run of 114 episodes ran from 1940-1958 and it is still produced.

MOON LAND

One family holiday on the edge of Wales.
Sun rose inland there and prowled along
the village street into a tight-curved bay,
its rocks and pools and narrow breadth
with more coves a run or swim beyond.

Twice daily, we would walk a curling lane,
from broom-hedged chalet past cottages
and a beery pub. Mackerel, cod and herring
on the slipway, crab in baskets and, once,
two lobsters we bought and killed and ate.

An echoey beachfront café down the coast.
The juke box was jammed on Peter Sarstedt
and babbling families occupied a few tables.
Chair legs scraped the floor and a small TV
in one corner showed men in bubble suits.

They were bouncing on a different beach,
where the tide was so far out none of us
could see it. Later, a quarter moon waxed
above us on the terrace and we conjured
dry dust settling on a Sea of Tranquillity.

OOOOPS

It is after midnight and blossom on the pear
outside my window has changed to wool,
thanks to moonlight seeping through clouds
and across the open space where two rows
of suburban gardens back on to each other.

In the distance, somewhere beyond London,
past the city's lights and the tart stains
of too many creatures and not enough air,
there is a deep silence of planets and stars
hanging like fruit, out of reach and over-ripe.

So, is it work for farmers, to travel further
than their eyes can see or comprehend?
Would they go there to cultivate new worlds,
leaving the skid row of home far behind,
with its diminishing minerals and tired fields?

Or do the hunters still have their day to come,
armed and dangerous, with space-age equivalents
of guns and blades? Spirits watching over them
may not engender respect, but rely on destiny,
staring out into the dawn, grey-eyed and strong.

The sky will never fall the way we expect.
All that immensity will settle quite suddenly,
moving a few fractions to crush us all.
One continuous slice of luck keeps me awake
on this side of the glass and looking up.

GHAZAL: MOON

Neil Armstrong bounced and pronounced on the moon.
My 7th birthday staring at the moon.

Wrack in runes, out of tune, 'I nearly swooned.'
What does it mean to be ruled by the moon?

Shot white wax in the blueblack sky,
smooth skin, cool music, full moon.

'Pull and swell and river to oblivion,'
a barren woman contemplates the moon.

The Forum's disco-backlit: green, red, blue.
Through Colosseum arches, the scimitar moon.

Opalescent, moody, multiply tattooed,
selenotropic sisters praise the moon.

Old, Snow, Sap, Grass, Milk, Rose, Thunder Moon.
Green Corn, Fruit, Harvest, Frost, Long Night Moon.

In a poem composed in Greek, the sea
is slivered, silvered, fingers of the moon.

While haply she sits upon her throne,
dull lovers, soul-split, weep beneath the moon.

Wolf, Snow, Worm, Pink, Flower, Strawberry Moon.
Buck, Corn, Harvest, Hunter's, Beaver, Cold Moon.

A perfect curlicue of Irish butter.
A lake of wavy onyx, mirrored moon.

'It is not the moon, I tell you.'
But yes it is, it is, always, the moon.

SELENOTROPE

Legend has it that
Li Po leaped into the moon's
reflection, late night

drunk, disordered on
wine and poems, the river
dark and delicious.

Scholars maintain it
was cirrhosis or poison,
a toxic Taoist

elixir brewed of
mercury and misplaced hopes
for longevity.

Longevity. Ha.
Who hasn't, lugubrious,
brooded over it.

Who wouldn't want to
embrace that satellite's sad
light on a dark night

of the soul, the space
between real and possible
grown astronomical.

PIERROT LUNAIRE

That day, the moon ceased to be
your mum's sickle curse, dad's
crystal ball, God's peeping hole

That day, the moon turned
a child's bleak universe
into a stage bursting
with unmatched lexicons

Dvorak's *New World Symphony*
set the tone as you watched
Armstrong take baby steps
on earth's orbital body

That day, you skipped away
from childhood's pitch. Invented
a *Sprechstimme*. Rehearsed
your part in life's show

Fifty years on, a live
apocrypha, you excise
words from your score

The first one to go is *speech*
(how it swirls up in thin air)
The last one has to be *voice*

ALONE WITH THE DARK

The sky has its passengers
so many are fallen past the white
—Jill Jones

An odour of seaweed   A whiff of oil   Open space from littoral to ocean   Earth to firmament   Day a sunken boulder on a sandbar   The horizon lies flat on your hand   Underfoot squeaky sand   Plastic scraps to glide onto   A dead seal alive with maggots   Night glass water   The milky way stitches you to the cosmos   Shhh   A chirp   Blue moon thrust against the sky   You lower your gaze   The sea froths at the river's mouth   A taste of salt   Spray and spume on the surface of the water   Whitecaps everywhere   You dive   Surface   Paddle   Plough the water as you would *wordsoil*   Strike the waves harder and harder   You are a rider of white horses rolling in as the storm gathers momentum and the sun slowly climbs on its upward course   *Schimmelreiterin*   You are a prose poem on the make   *Stimmung*   Seething semiotic flux   Not gravid amniote   *Allant-toi*   Fuzzy-wuzzy wavelets   Horsehair in *aqualune*   *Lunaqua*   *Chevaux de frise*   Friesland   *Mijn platte land*   *Belaqua*   Whetting stone   Cutting cold   You are flayed alive   *El desdichada*   Sheer *mise en abyme*   An eclipse   Washed ashore memory   *Fussig* pebbles   Pummice   Porous skin   Papyrus   *Pailles de papier*   Flick flicker   The sky catches on fire   Tongues of pink violet crimson lemon orange butter blue   Plumes of sea green   Elderflower ash   Ember rain   *Schimmel*   *Argent*   *Alloi*   *Hors la loi*   Ululation   Black sun shining bright

ONE SMALL STEP FOR [A] MAN

The speech is rehearsed but misheard or misspoken, a misquotation of itself, and already it is 1.27 seconds gone, history already made. As grey shifts to grey, its slap of shadow on shadow like the last card played, I feel I've won something bigger than the world, though I can't say what. Perhaps it's the key to a glowing dome on a grey frontier; my own ray-gun; a trusty dog in a fishbowl helmet; a silver rope to tie me to the stars: perhaps it's a scrapbook full of pictures of the Earth, with everyone shading their eyes and waving; a pocketful of souvenir coins to spend on the dark side of the Moon; a chip off the stone that hangs in the night sky, balancing on a shared hopeful breath. I have no speech writer, so I blub amazement, misquoting my Dan Dare heart. Tomorrow morning, I'll take delivery of moonlight, hang it from the ceiling amongst Airfix Apollos; but by then it will be 1.27 seconds old, already unsure of who may have said what, the charcoal smudge of stars and stripes.

EARTHRISE

Even in the digital age there are no photographs. While Chinese robots film each other, flirting behind the Moon, we hide in plain sight in a chintzy café, all our devices switched off or set to silent. It takes time to relearn lines, and our lips are out of sync with our words, each pleasantry shuffling between us 1.27 seconds late. On the wall is a print of *Earthrise*, back in fashion but adrift from its old meanings, and you say that maybe these days the most important things are those which go unrecorded; not the lightbulbs at all, but the wires that connect them and jolt them into life. I recall something similar from Virginia Woolf, but by the time I frame my response, your next delayed sentence arrives and I am looking into the Sun. There are no photographs, and I am burned out and floating as the room rotates, its retro stylings drifting into deep distance, its teaspoons and tip jar glimmering like dust in the night sky. We are quarter of a million miles apart, with no recourse but to compare our favourite Moons: mine is almost full, round but for the breath of longing; yours is gibbous, for the way it makes you kiss space.

WAXING

I.

Song net. Flag scar. Youth in ascent. Regular
but transient reunions. Once repped hearts
from Taipei to Tampines, this pockmarked aspect,
this loony tune of a nightlight would clip your ears,
said grandma, if you pointed at it. And sour your
marriage prospects. Some deity. Still, a lepak foil
to the diligent day, less kancheong spider, more
rabbit den. Churning out herbal highs for the celestial
classes, far enough away from the hoi polloi. Refuge
for abused wives. Safety as exile. We've been there.

II.

Did he or did he not? One small snafued soundbite for (a) man a 'poetic slip' says BBC (3 June 2009). Poetic lunacies since: flatearthers; antivaxxers; moondenialists; fakenews. Expertise just another cry for attention without the beauty filters. Something tidal about the way Skywalker has a bigger budget than skywalkers. Fiction as fixture. Peeled away from limits, taken one giant leap across the uncanny valley of what might be made up. A small step from scaling the impossible to the impossibility of scale. And then sea levels, coral bleaching, herd collapse, scarcity: profit. See how it goes.

WANING

        how   verbs   shift   weight
   seen   stu died   land ed set tled
left   to wish   they had been
  clean   en ough
               to join   here
                                in Lunia

look how the
                  smoke
    from burning
            mountains
                      eyebrows
            the blue
                  mask
                            of   history
there
       the ball   where all
              began
                      un
                      til sur
                                passed
    by some
          by some   sur
   vived
                  succumbed to

the air
    here   made
  to order   safe for   the young
      in small
                  doses
we will need
     all we can save   where we are
          going.

FOOTPRINT

The inlet is dry   so dry
where last year this valley was soft
with deep lament of swan song
I now walk a moonscape   harsh and dry
pock-holed and wide   grieve
lost world of liquid mystery
Fish traps   holding pools
stones placed long ago   exposed
their quiet lines
kicked by cattle

Surrounded not by life   but sand
I am the first man
on the moon   we tread
where he assumes none have gone
before   we leave
our trace

1 a.m.

Great Southern, Western Australia

1 a.m.   unsleeping
in a home still not my own

everything strange

new abundance
of silence

outside windows
a wild darkness.

I step out in a T-shirt   skin
calling to moist summer air

no wind   Marri tree shape of an enormous
absence   a sculpted void

backlit by something I cannot understand
its uncountable brilliance

each point of light the precise white
of longing.

TRACE

The moon – a seemingly barren rock – may actually be a treasure trove of rare resources vital to the Earth's future.
—NASA Jet Propulsion Laboratory

How long does a footprint last,
the partial, seven-striped tread
snapped by Buzz, beamed
round a gaping world?
On the moon, your guess
is as good as the next.
Is the solar wind favourable,
will an asteroid strike?
Will the man with the plan
for a mining shaft in the sea
play golf instead,
leave Tranquillity salinated,
the apple on the tree?

AFTER ILLUMINATION

What if those certainties eclipse,
when you round the corner, slow pace,
and the white glare of a half-moon off-axis
blanches out the stars, stains the sky,
blurs clouds like masses on an ultrasound
haunting your sleep and waking?
What use perspective now, a knowledge of phases?
Say all you like about lifespans, transience,
the dog days between one lit candle and another.
The light we make, that we recognise,
has no lunar calendar, no times or dates.

MOON, O

        true moon, if you love us,
     give us nothing. Blank us. Don't
disclose a wink of water, not a glitter-speck of ore—
       nothing to raise a twinkle
    in the futures market's eye. Chaste
goddess (did you have an inkling, all this time, of our
cracked yearnings, how we would madden ourselves,
        how girn in your direction vaguely?)
         stay that way—a glimpse
of pure negation, so not us, not ours, so unwarmed
      to our touch, unstirred by the least
         wind or whim.
        Don't let us think, not
     for a moment, we can have you.
Leave those toddler-suited astronauts slack-dangled
        in their old home movies,
like marionettes in the wardrobe,
a childhood we'd better forget. Leave the tangled
tracks of our million-dollar toys where they crawled
     to a halt amidst the perfect pointlessness
       of you. O bleachy-
skinned cool mistress, arsenic complexion, dead-
    pan geisha unmoved by our high romance,
     all the shadow-puppetry
      we made of you, O
pocked and harrowed cheek, no wonder,
those rough-sleeping nights on the sidewalk of space, O
      never really mistress,
   tell us to sling our hook, to blast
and fizzle off, remember we've got family at home.

SKY SPACE

    1.   Egg within egg within egg,
sphere within sphere
                      cracked open
by Copernicus ... What we found outside
was next to nothing.
                      Year by year,
look further, and the vertigo will deepen.

    2.   Where does *sky* become *space*? When
did this happen?
                      The first high flight
to break the illusion of blue, to see the air
that we mistook for clarity
                      as a tide,
a shoreline, foam receding at your feet?

    3.   We had always had night, and stars,
another revelation
                      as different from day
as dream from waking. In both, the sense
that *it*, the mystery, is drawing close.
                      The sky
meanwhile has gone immeasurably far away.

    4.   Praise be, the new psalmist might sing,
to the radio telescope array,
                      the thin skies
of the Atacama, those rapt watchers,
for they show us the heights
                      into which
we might fall, depths to which we might rise.

BUZZ 1

I like the way Buzz Aldrin
at the end of all that science
and wild collaboration

ate and drank his small communion
privately, without a priest,
not quite a quarter million

miles from off the earth
and how he later half-recanted
(though smiling still to think

the first meal ever on the moon
was made from bread and wine),
regretting just a little that

the sacrament had been
a Christian one alone
and so began to name the rest,

Muslims, Jews and *Animists,*
Atheists, Agnostics,
a list implying all the others,

Buddhists, Hindus, Sikhs and *Pagans,*
all of us he knew would share
on starry nights his taste for wonder.

BUZZ 2

On the night before the splashdown
addressing his attentive millions
Buzz Aldrin found himself compelled

without a fuss to quote Psalm 8—
the good bit, mentioning how God
had cleverly 'ordained' the 'moon

and stars'. 'The work of Thy fingers',
Buzz intoned. 'What is man
that Thou art mindful of him?'

King David asked, alone one night,
considering the heavens.
'Good question,' I'm inclined to chirp.

'And what about the fingers, eh?
Did they have a thumb to work with,
opposable and dextrous?'

As somewhere near I hear a voice
illimitably deep and calm:
Easy on the details, boy.

Enjoy the metaphor!

NEIL ARMSTRONG LEAPS

Like a raindrop bouncing
From the surface of a road,
Like a cat jumping
At a wren in a hedge,
Like an idea tangoing
From his head to ours
About distance, and closeness
And the amount of air
We all need to leap in.

UNCLE CHARLIE'S MOON

I recall this: his braces
Like a kind of punctuation
Down his shirt. His cap, flat
As a pit pond. His anger.

He points at the distant
Bike lamp of the moon.
'They're nivver theer,
Ian lad. Nivver.' He shakes

His head, coughs, spits.
He can't hear Buzz Aldrin
Shouting 'Charlie! We're here!'
But I can, Charlie. I can.

NONNO

Rarely moved—the creases of his walnut face—
except at our pranks, when we would have to pause
to check whether the deltas of his lips signalled
smile or grimace; or when, under diamond-dust stars,
he stirred the butterfly in me with stories
Jupiters away from Janet and John.

Unmoved, it seemed, in that evening yard
astride the chair, hat and waistcoat as always, hands
folded atop the cane—all implied in near-darkness—
the red disc of his cigar a slow pulsar
on the blank square of the cantina doorway.
In the street the one feeble bulb, a tungsten moon,
flickered its orbits of moths, prolonging shadows
where the village huddled

round the glow-tube of its first TV
and coaxed him out to watch: *the man on the moon.*
His eyes, as ours, fixed on that screen—
the bloated magnesium of spacesuits,
those planetary heads; and Armstrong, Armstrong
hopping mad.

I couldn't read him then.
The way the skin-pleats gathered over his eyes.
How, humourless, he gave the last laugh
the only laugh of his I heard—cranked out
that it was all some trick with mirrors.
Why, getting up, he broke the long-unbroken
time of retiring, turning his back
extinguished the dull ember
of his cheroot. In those long years after
never told stories again.

Nonno—Grandad; cantina—wine cellar.

BARRIER

(Cairns, Australia)

In thin flat hues we see it drift
past the porthole—borne beneath us
on a microscope-slide of ocean:

amoebae of greener blue frilled
with the white fibrillae of surf—or
is it bright sulphate in a Petri dish

precipitating brown pancakes
of copper? Inorganic. Organic.
Images can swing both ways

for this hybrid of germ and rock,
these rods and spits of yeast
and bacillus. This is Life

made all the more strange
for being viewed from two
billion years up the food chain

through a lens of travel. Zoom in
and trigger-fish suck each tiny jelly
from its coral cup. Zoom out

and satellites make a thin
uneven curve that puts Australia
in parenthesis. Yes—we can

do all that. But this is our future
on a thread. A glimpse of our
Earth-child learning its chemistries

with no one to teach the lesson.

MOON LANDING

At the front of the primary school classroom, the spacecraft's legs stand like fixed pointers and the figure we see through the small television's static and blur makes a weird cameo. His words sound under-rehearsed as we imagine speaking inside a helmet—he inspects dirt, occlusion, dark air. The earth spins absent-mindedly below his feet as we watch the enclosed, exotic space and consider the prospect of walking with a bouncing gait. Soon someone will try it in the yard. We imagine ourselves transformed, despite the dust bunnies on the floor and the scratchy blackboard's usual ladder of sums. Later, during our lesson on collective nouns, someone will posit *a blaze of astronauts* as the teacher frowns. While we wait to become more than we are, Armstrong's voice hesitates in our ears.

MEADOWS

Space seethes with planets and stars. If our ideas were brighter, we might shine in the future's dark firmament, adorning the world with green millennia. The deserts admonish, reminding us of unchecked winds and aeons of absence; recent narratives are sand sifted by idle fingers; scorpions crawl from their holes. We hear Neil Armstrong's words rebound—there's no common language in the expanding universe. A spiral arm points at lovers under the moon. They walk together into a wide sense of beauty—as if heaven's meadows have tumbled to the ground or, like Orion and Cassiopeia, they're painted in the sky.

SPACE COUTURE

i.
Stepping from the spacecraft, Armstrong dons a dramatic Extravehicular Mobility Unit made from layers of teflon-coated silica-fiber cloth and a woven form of stainless steel. Tailored by seamstresses from a bra and girdle assembly line in Frederica, Delaware, ILC Industries have combined unlikely materials and textures to striking new effect. Tough but appealingly cuddly, the suit comes with matching gloves and helmet, attached at points accented with red metal rings. Entry to the lunar space suit is through a tasteful rear pressure-sealing zipper made from brass with a neoprene gasket. The suit weighs 180 pounds, or just 30 on the surface of the moon; the figure-hugging design a triumph of craft-culture handiwork over engineering.

ii.
Bobbins spinning, pressure feet trilling down the aluminised plastic, the seamstresses are fashioning a place for themselves in history. They gather together twenty-one gossamer layers like onion skins and stitch them together. I sit at my grandmother's Singer sewing machine and fill the bobbin with silver thread. Placing the hem of the dress under the Singer's shiny foot, I press down on the pedal and the machine speeds around the circle of the skirt. As the television blares the anniversary of the moon landing, I ask her what she remembers. She puts down her cup of tea and smiles, 'waving at the moon on my front lawn; squinting to see if Neil Armstrong was waving back.'

ASTRONAUT ICE-CREAM

At the Smithsonian giftshop, I weigh you down with freeze-dried Neapolitan ice-cream. Pink stripe. Chocolate stripe. White stripe in between—a kind of no-woman's land. Keeping chocberry possibilities at bay. I've never liked the middle band of vanilla ice-cream, have always eaten it last. It reminds me of cheap scented candles or essence in a cake. 'Vanilla—like sex on Thursdays,' I once said. You didn't laugh. I'm not sure if it was because it was a Thursday. In the National Air and Space museum you tell me I'll probably be your last lover. And I spend the afternoon worrying about 'probably'. And whether 'probably' means 'possibly', which would make it more possible. Or likely. And why you didn't just say 'likely'. You drag me around the 17,000 space artifacts but you are most interested in the Apollo 11 objects. Buzz's helmet appears to be your favourite, but I'm fascinated with the object labelled 'Pouch, Storage with Roll-on Urine Cuffs' and wonder why anyone would want to keep the 'Fecal Collection Assembly'. You are delighted to find the astronauts left 93 bags of poo, pee and puke on the moon, but I don't think that's very friendly—eco or otherwise. You can't say, 'we come in peace' and then leave excrement as your parting gift. We ask the museum curator where we can find the astronaut ice-cream. He tells us it was rejected for flight because it was too crumbly for zero gravity—the astronauts had butterscotch pudding instead. So, I want a refund for false advertising. The man in the giftshop says, 'In space, no-one can hear your ice-scream' with a wink, and I say 'probably' and think it's very likely.

SPACE RACE, 1969

Thirteen, between worlds, I waited
to wear the big shirts of men. The bare legs
of girls made me restless. The clock
on the classroom wall said wait, wait,
wait for the next world.

In bed at night, I heard
apples thump the ground
as fruit divorced the tree. Gravity
made little sense—how did it find
apples to pull them down? How did
a force invisible & untouchable hold
all things at once? 'Gravity comes
from the Earth's mass,' my teacher said,
as if that resolved the problem.

I wanted the bruised apple to
refasten to its branch.
I wanted my father to remarry my mother.
I wanted five boosters—escape velocity.
I wanted to shed my stages.
I wanted balanced equations & precision.
I wanted the atmosphere's rough kiss.
I wanted remote orbits & then
my brilliant, homeward blaze.
I wanted to choose my world.
I wanted Armstrong's lightness on the moon.

FORBIDDEN PLANET

On Altair 4, planet of the Krell,
9,200 nuclear reactors
power the 'Plastic Educator,'
which converts ideas into matter.
The Plastic Educator also—
unknown to the Krell—makes
creatures of lust, rage,
unreason (the mind
within the mind). The Krells
perish from super-high-tech
projections of themselves.

In this movie from 1956,
a flying saucer's crew all speak
English with an American accent.
The crew—all white 'superior
specimens of manhood'—escape Altair
as it flashes into cinders.

Dystopia of old sci-fi displaced
dystopia here (Americas within
America). The President prays
to an obsolete future & its return.

Give us this day our daily
tweet—a vortex of confetti,
karaoke of grudge-songs.
Give us our Plastic
Educators to cast
a collective Id, monstrous,
in the orange glow of laser fire.

THE LITTLE OLD LADIES OF NASA

old-maidy   matronly   devil-finds-work
crafts from once-upon-times when women
knew their place (under   beneath   below)
when yawn-making inchesfeetyards   of blankets
and scarves   leapt   from un-idle hands
transform into a spool a thread a skein   a square
connected to another square   a net   a rope-core
memory-web to cast the eagle lunarwards
to its high eyrie   ripple-stitch   shell-stitch
one-zero-one   skirting the magnets   puff-stitch
post-stich last-laugh kickass knit-one-purl-two
weave copper wire around or through   chain-stitch
granny-stitch   one small stitch for   womankind
plait a moonmap   knot-tight into tranquillity

Read-only software called core rope memory, used in the Apollo Guidance computers, was woven by female workers. It was known as LOL memory. (Little Old Lady)

MAP

Animated isobars swoop in from the sea, peppered with arrows showing wind direction, shadows of clouds across the land, bands of rain approaching from the west. Our species blows out of Africa in all directions, hunting the herds, seeking rich pasture; resting and tilling the land until dust-storms of hunger or malice pick us up like houses in a typhoon, bowl us onwards. We are the children of Israel, driven into slavery and led out of Egypt, wandering in the desert, weeping by the rivers of Babylon, Ruth in tears amid the alien corn. We are Europeans spreading like contagion in oak ships and steel superiority, herding thousands of Africans against the prevailing winds to lands where they will harvest wealth for their owners. We are American settlers lined up across the prairie, where a pistol-shot starts us racing on horses, in wagons, to grab and stake and claim, pushing the First Nation before us like a wave; ploughing and planting for a few generations until the wind carries away the soil and we become Okies in our piled-high trucks, faces turned hunger-hard towards the setting sun. We are the human debris of the hurricane of the second world war, families with push-carts and prams, trudging west; we are the flash-flood rivers of people flowing from India to Pakistan, from Pakistan to India; we are the kicked-up dust of all the wars since. People gusted into piles like autumn leaves, the isobars shifting again, coming this way.

INTERIOR OF THE GARDEN I

IN THE GARDEN OF LOVE I SAW THE TOWERING CLIFFS, THE TRANQUIL SEA. EASTWARD INTO SHADOW, LEANED THROUGH TIME AND DREAMED. ANOTHER PARADISE—FOUND WHOLE ORCHARDS AND GOLDEN FRUITS—THOUGH EXPOSED AND AN AIRLESS COUNTRY, THE ANIMALS THE FORMS CHANGED. IN THE COOL OF THE DAY, OVER SUNLIT PLANES MY SHADOW, STEPPED ACROSS AND STEPPED LIGHTLY. SWEET VINES, PEACE IN THE VALLEYS. IN THE GARDEN THE BEASTS AND THE BIRDS. ABOVE—METEORS, THE WARRING EARTH. AFTER MILLENNIA WAS RETURNED: TO HISTORY AND BLOOD DELIVERED. BACK, IN THE OLD HOME. GRIEF, THE IRRETRIEVABLE AGE. THE WHITE WAGONS DRAWING WEST.

INTERIOR OF THE GARDEN II

NEW YORK, 15 APRIL

Dearest,
It seemed momentous, our leaving, but no one was there to see us go, at least I haven't remembered that. Everyone says to witness a lift off is a powerful thing to see. The feel of the raw power pushing against your chest, your heart. It makes you know you're alive doesn't it?

It's hardly possible to imagine your tears at the edge of fate last year, chance pressing its blunt nose into the palm of your hand, as if you might have more to offer. I don't want to lose that memory of the snow seared by the phone's flash, our faces fading into the dark. I'm remembering the risk he took in coming with us at all, the atmospheres that waited for us hostile, toxic. It was a bleak journey with the light of the car the only barrier between us and darkness.

This time we sleep through the night as if it was simple. Last year, I lost count of how many times we woke in that same hospital room Jackie O slept in, the corner one with a fine view of Manhattan stretching below us. What was she suffering from? I didn't think to ask. I suppose I didn't want to know about the affliction of others. Sometimes it's best if it's a pain individually shared, the surgeon tells me.

There is the pink moon, it's like a blooming. A single breast suspended in the sky I might have thought before, when all my thoughts were splintered. Each idea asunder, just like us, two sisters separated by an ocean. For both of us the moon is full and out of reach. But look now, the blossoms are out and everything seems rosy.
Yours,

CAMBRIDGE, 27 APRIL

Dearest,
Since we parted I've watched the sun rise and set here on the other side of the world. This time the dawn is a soft grey and the birdsong is like a ghosting. It's hard to avoid jet lag although you've told me to disregard the old time.

How is it that this new world so filled with promise has such blanks in it? I want to look for the footsteps, trodden long before my shadow fell here. Don't wait for the future, my son says, it's because he's impatient and he wants to make things happen. He and his brother want to know what it means to be quoted, as though it's something magical.

I've been hovering at this in between time for hours, it's not dark or light, day or night. I should feel unsettled but I like it here enough to quash the fear of exhaustion or misery. I want to imagine a view of this tiny planet, green and blue. They say that forty million birds have disappeared over the past fifty years. People are glueing themselves to the pulse points of the city in desperation. Imagine this morning slipping through your fingers, the impossibility of bird song, imagine the loss of atmosphere and the leap that will send me drifting through the air like dust.

We haven't spoken about the eclipse, is that what we should call it? The orbs of both sun and moon erased, leaving a dark hole in the sky. It's only natural, I tell you, but that's the past and it makes you shudder. All your thoughts are about the next sunrise, watching it glint around the edges of the horizon. There's a satisfaction in knowing you have found the finest place to watch it, even if it is unbearably fragile. The slightest sound or light will shatter this illusion of difference between here and there, now and then, even between us.
Yours,

SEWING THE MOON

No matter how I tried
I fumbled, red cotton
                                 Wrapped around my finger
                                                                      Undone.

stupid girl the cross-stitch genius
                                   Announced
                                                                  Disgusted

How could she know my mother was perfect?
                                   At cross stitch, crochet and knitting
And, I a failure at them all
                               My inheritance of the skill definitely in doubt
Must be a half blood
                                   Obviously not a weaver

Stand in the hall she decreed
The genius guardian of red cotton cross stitch
                                   And then it happened

That one giant leap for all of mankind
That first step on the moon

Not a sound but the TV in the room

I'd failed at cross stitch

I missed it all.

      That night in the dark I slipped outside
The willow tree danced in the breeze
                The man in the moon smiled back

            A cloud
                  passed by

A WINTER MOON

I wanted to write a poem, soft and round

like the moon, full of light
Dependable and there
Even if hidden by clouds

I wanted to write a poem, soft and round

Something magic
About maps in the sky
Ancestors longings and belongings

But I can't sleep at night
I am restless, tossing and turning
With the tidal pull on my circadian rhythm

I fear for this place
Our earth, I fear for all that gives life
Our rivers, our oceans, our trees

I wanted to write a poem, soft and round

But I cry tears at night when I go outside
My heart is broken
My tears could fill dying rivers

The world has become jagged

I'm sorry, I would have liked to write you a poem

like the moon,
soft and round

LUNAR, NAKED

There's something naked about it   the light
and then our cloaked flesh was there

There's always something precise about it
though we know it's dusty

It's always like a dream   looking back at you
as if someone had   been standing there

No, not those men in their cages
with their flag   their boots bruising the regolith
with a deed   an imprint   one flag (one too many)
    a scratch on the universe's eye

Wanting to be modern   they left their rubbish
    (that's always modern)

July 21, it was winter here   cold as moon shade
as one stone shines on   another stone

There are people who still believe
it was all done on a movie set   perhaps like
    all our lives   so   what do
we believe   within the epic of spaceglow

If they had been naked   is that
    what was needed   if they'd sifted
lunar dust through their open hands
    their literal skin

GIANT STEPS, ATLANTIC RECORDS SD 1311, 1960

I start from one point and go as far as possible.
—John Coltrane

Coltrane's still playing out there   still on
    a solo run   with the band   though there's
no sound in space vacuum   sound waves
can move through   clouds   of gas between stars
    hush into the outer gasps   of atmospheres

         Albert Ayler once said:
'John was like a visitor   to this planet.
   He came in peace   and he left in peace.'

It's all about time.   Music is time.
Coltrane once said: 'I want more of
    the sense of   the expansion of   time.'

Amongst interstellar vapour   in the whole
    of every moon   light travel   of billion years
kaleidoscoping chords   sheets of stars
    changing   and burning   still

      that first track   on Tuesday 5th May, 1959
John Coltrane   Tommy Flanagan   Paul Chambers
Art Taylor   Atlantic Studios New York
    two weeks after the final sessions of *Kind of Blue*

      Archie Shepp once said:
'Coltrane showed   the rest of us
we had to have   the stamina   to sustain
those long flights.'
         And still playing   on

SINGULARITY

Staring back through that *magnificent desolation*
to this devilled blue globe, one dome suspended in light,
the other obscured by the shadow of where you stood;
immersed as you were in light particles
from long-dead stars, did you wonder
at our seemingly eternal journey,
cycling over and over from light
to dark to light? Reflecting on Earth:
seeing 'home' for the first time in that vast
perspective at once vivid and spectral; this silenced beauty
turning slowly over its own desolate truth:
the enormity of its one persisting challenge—
to somehow find our allied humanity
—a singular planetary alignment
as subtly elusive as one
perfect surface reflection.
As great and bungled.
As necessary as the light
we feed on, as desperate
to repel the dark, over and
over to separate and break us
apart from the spectre of some alternative reality,
time folded in on itself, suspending us in an-
other perpetual virtual truth
and the hovering ghosts of
what could have been.

BLESSED AMONGST LUNACIES

I: A living room in west Clare, Ireland—21 July 1969

Hands grasping at the grey screen, agasp—
my brother's face round and bright
as the moon behind, reflecting back
the blue light, this rock around which I orbited,
magnetically attracted & repelled according to
his mercurial moods.

II: Lake Toba, Sumatra, Indonesia—September 1993

Lake-water oddly blood-temperature, viscous
& deathly dark. Floating naked on my back
within a lapping galaxy; a slick touch—gasp
& panicked turn into that inky, airless realm,
silent but for a muffled thundering; pivoting,
kicking instinctively for light: guided only by stars;
legs still thrusting when they struck shore—
two black wings thrashing in the cage
of my heart, a bone-sliver poking
through silver-pricked black.

III: A medical facility in Sydney, Australia—November 2004

Over the glowing dome of my bare abdomen,
a mottled landscape laid out in grainy greys.
Gasp—at that alien face looming,
a tiny foot poised against black space.
A giant leap   into uncharted territory:
struck by the light of my first son, unadulterated then,
but so often since eclipsed   by the fear
of what on Earth we will leave them.

NOSTALGIA

Jackals howl from three points of the compass
as planes fly overhead in dizzying spirals, the moon
has been carved in half, her craters jutting out in profile—
who knows which plane the man is roaming on,
and whether he carries a handful of earth
to remind him.

The clouds do not know if they are coming or going,
caught in the gears as we try to disengage at 1 a.m.—
now tucked away behind a blanket of vapour she is
a dark shadow against an even darker sky—
a window to nowhere and everywhere, almost
like a black hole.

MOON IN TOKYO

I thought I had seen you in all your guises
but tonight you hover behind a velvet veil,
surrounded by waves of a gossamer halo—
veins and bruises of a deeper blue, as though your body
once carried oceans and rivers, and now you are left
with only their spectres.

I thought I had seen you the way you see me,
illumined by your light and easy to read,
emergent silver strands curving through my hair—
creases appear like cautious writing, as though my body
tries to discern space and time, and I show you me
as I wish to see you.

I thought I had seen you dressed every which way,
but I was not prepared for the Tokyo sky.

WHAT WE DIDN'T KNOW

The last day of school before summer
we didn't have class, just listened to the principal's speech
and went home while it was still morning.
Y and I met to go to K's house to play.
Then K's mother offered to take us to lunch
at a noodle shop nearby.
She ordered for the three of us *kitsune udon*, fox noodles,
paid in advance and left us to the summer's freedom.
Delicious smells of soy sauce and bonito flakes
filled the air as we waited.
Then we noticed the TV rambling on,
a dark picture, the simultaneous translator's Japanese
following a series of invisible actions.
It happened just before noon.
Big steps, big deal, strong arms, buzzing a light year.
We were eleven years old, with no sense of success or failure,
keen on our summer big beetle hunting and daily swim
in the dirty school pool.
We went on eating our *udon*, not making much of the giant leap
for mankind, then left the shop.
Our steps were into summer days, our trifling future,
our own respective destinies.

K died the following year of leukemia,
leaving nothing but some lost steps in our minds.

MOTHER MOON

Visiting a friend in Laguna, New Mexico,
we went out into the night, full moon deadly bright,
coyotes howling in the distance.
Can you believe some guys actually went there? I asked, looking up at the moon.
That was a bad move, my friend said.
You should not step on your mother, you know.

Mother Moon, eternally beautiful and loving,
Shining at night, embracing us small creatures on the surface of the earth.
Mother Moon, cool, pale and tender.

No steps should have been taken,
no national flag should have been stuck on you,
no stones should have been brought back.

Something deadly began then on the earth.
Neon signs of neo-liberalism now ravage
what is left for us here on this planet.

Sea of Tranquility is disturbed. Big time.
Our Pacific is collapsing. Big time.

SMALL STEPS

Christmas Eve 1968 and, orbiting the Moon, men
watch Earth rise, its blue-veined surface halved
by darkness. Tiny, to the crew of Apollo 8, it seems
to float and spin eight billion of us into our futures.

I was fifteen, had published my first poem, met
the man I'd marry. Life was exciting: anything could happen.
Summer landed Apollo11. In love, we watched
white jump-suited men lift, float, descend and step;
lift, float, descend and step across pale soil
inside a black and white TV with wooden doors
that my mother snapped shut when she said
we'd had enough. But, out there
they kept floating, light as their spirits, bright as our wonder.
We stood in the back yard under northern stars,
trying to sense what was changing.
My grandfather muttered it wasn't reet –
that tinkerin' wi' yonder would flummox the weather.

Armstrong, the man from a Border clan, had made
'one small step'; others had followed so, one day, we might too.
Snug at the centre of our new world, no imagined
threat of storms, heatwaves, or floods could shake us.

Sometime between then and now we touched down,
realised what mankind's giant leaps brought with them,
saw how far each one of us would need to travel

just to keep our own lives spinning,
to keep the planet we loved, happily habitable:

knew our own small steps were many and still to come.

UP TO US

'God gave us the gift of life; it is up to us to give ourselves the gift of living well.'
—Voltaire

Most of what we lost out there is still orbiting:
a tool bag, pliers, a wrench, several cameras,
a thermal blanket, someone's toothbrush,
bits of spent rockets, launch canisters, an astronaut's glove
that took off during the first spacewalk.

Then there are the millions of particles, too small to be monitored,
more powerful on impact than a bullet moving at 30,000 mph:
flakes of frozen coolant, flecks of paint, propellant tank fragments
raining down on Japanese sailors, a walking woman,
unsuspecting camels, any of us, any time.

We're trying to bring it down with a harpoon
the size of a pen, a net, a de-orbit sail, our telescopes
sweeping what used to be clear. Ten flags still stand
on the Moon, colours faded, countries wiped clean.
Plans germinate to mine rare metal, elements, water,

on the dark side. While, from the other direction,
four billion years ago, meteorites may have showered Earth
with molecules of water, carbon and phosphorus oxoacids –
natural litter, not exactly seeds, but all that was needed to
give us life.

VACUUM PACK

Begin with metal pole and flag, spring-loaded
to wow and flutter without the benefit
of air. To underline the point, surround it
with the inexpungible prints of small steps
taken in oversize boots. A replica,
in gold, of an olive branch. *We came in peace
for all mankind.* A plaque, stuck to the module.
Medals left behind. Boots, having made their mark
discarded. The tube and plastic covering
for the flag, also discarded. Overshoes,
ditto. When you hurl fifty tonnes of metal,
flesh, plastic, fabric, food and water so far,
you don't need it all back. Take some rocks instead.
Two items left for each rock taken seems fair
exchange. If, like a careless tourist, you drop
film canisters, filters, lenses, then why not
leave the whole camera, once its job is done.
Hasselblad, TV camera, cables, all.
Now that the rocks are seized, throw away the scoop,
the tongs, the scales. Life support packs, no longer
needed, left behind. Making a final mark,
four sick bags—status of contents not listed—
four urine collection assemblies, all used,
four defecation collection devices.
The special astronaut diapers will go back,
stinking, although an entire lunar module
descent stage gathers moondust and cosmic rays.
We will plan one day for an expedition
to check what we left behind for signs of life.

THE ASTROPHYSICIST TO HIS LOVE

Under a curve of black sky, frost settles
on grass, crystal by crystal, glinting back
at the spread and swirl of inconstant stars

Reach out and take my cold hand in yours

All those stars should fall inward like apples
down wells of gravity until they are
indistinguishable, crushed into each other

Hold me, because I am lonely and cold

All stars should fall but do not. With slowness
that a year cannot measure they drift apart
pushed by unseen stuff that fills empty space

Kiss my eyelids; I do not want to see

The thing that fills empty space is darkness,
unseen and pushing everything away
until darkness alone is left, brooding

Love me till this dark, these stars are gone.

NEIL AND BUZZ TWO-STEP AT TRANQUILITY

Despite myself, I'm moved by grainy footage
of two white men dancing to a silent soundtrack
witnessed by five hundred million souls.
I'm moved to watch them leave a plaque
'We come in peace'—the timeless self-deception
of the human race—scoop rocks into tin cans,
plant toppling flags, hopscotch and skip like girls,
while Houston flicks switches and lights cigars.
From then on everything seems moonwashed—
clothes, songs, furniture, detergent, cars—
as if we'd glanced back at the small blue marble
of ourselves and thought we'd made it
and could hover in our shiny capsules for ever,
fearless, playful, closer to the stars.

FATOUMATA KÉBÉ CLEANS UP

Into vastness   she brings her telescope
                         her PhD in space debris ~~~
[1]

~`   . .   l'astronomie, ma passion //

les rêves d'enfant /./   a child's dreams

//130 million pieces orbit earth at 8 kilometres per second//
c'est un milieu très masculin // a very masculine environment

       ' t'es noire, t'es une femme, t'es musulmane
                             t'es ceci, t'es cela //
you're black, a woman, muslim
                       you're this, you're that '

je travaille sur les événements de fragmentation
      //

//   -..   •   préserver l'environnement spatial

pour nous   for us   pour le futur
                     avant tout   above all

---

[1]

ORCHESTRINO

_____

NIETZSCHEAN

EXCELSITUDE

SPACEFARING

MICRONUCLEI

ABRACADABRA

LEGERDEMAIN

LUMINESCENT

SEMPITERNAL

TERRASPHERE

EJECTAMENTA

PIONEERSHIP

ORCHESTRINO is a double acrostic of 11 words, each of 11 letters, written in honour of the epigram uttered by Neil Armstrong, during his first steps upon the Moon, as the Commander of Apollo 11.

#DEARMOON

We upthrust
the full moon,
like the skull,
of some fool,
whom fondly
we mourners
might regale
by the grave:

'Alas—poor
mortals, who
remain yoked
to this earth.'

#DEARMOON is a poem written at the invitation of the billionaire Yusaku Maezawa, who plans to launch a crew of artists on a journey to the Moon, aboard a rocketship sponsored by SpaceX.

MOONDUST

Dust that no wind will abrade,
sharp-edged enough to shred
the soft tissue of throat and lungs,

dust with a static charge
so it floats in the airless dark
or brilliance of the sun,

dust made from a billion strikes
of meteors or the flakes
of rocks heated by solar flares

then shattered by the instant cold
of unlit space, dust that was old
before Earth's continents drifted,

dust, kicked up by the boot
of that first step, clings to the suit
enclosing the skin, bone, muscle

of a man composed of dust
who has returned to dust,
the moondust he stirred still settling.

VIOLATION

And now Chinese moon shots have reached the other side
where no rock band has ever played or ever will
there being no air to carry a raucous voice,
no Yellow River for a poet to drown in
attempting to embrace his vision of lost love.
Others will experiment with a money shot
for the triple goddess's imagined riches;
crater water frozen in perpetual dark,
veins of electrum, rare minerals for smart phones.

The maiden, the mother, the crone will stay hidden,
conspire with the sun in syzygy so spring tides
rise in the Bay of Fundy or a pounding heart
as a hunter glimpses a girl bathing naked
and his dogs drag down his antlered head by the throat,
starshine, sunshine, earthshine, moonshine glazed in his eyes
as this blue and white pebble still spins in the void.

VIEW FROM THE MOON, 1969

from this vast darkness, the black velvet
loneliness, suddenly it strikes me

that tiny pea, pretty and blue
marbled sphere of water and plate tectonics

turning in a hail of debris and chaos
my god, that little thing, so delicate

this photograph will surely make us
appreciate what we have

        caspian tiger
        lake pedder earthworm

        gastric-brooding frog
        levuana moth

        pyranean ibex
        christmas island pipistrelle

        western black rhinoceros
        bramble cay melomys

I put up my thumb and shut one eye
blot out the earth

VIEW FROM THE MOON, 1969 incorporates quotes from Neil Armstrong, Buzz Aldrin, James Irwin and Alexey Leonov and lists some of the species made extinct since 1969.

DEAR MOON

Yusaku Maezawa, entrepreneur and art collector,
has made a significant downpayment on a trip around the moon.
Ever since I was a kid, I have loved the moon very much.

Space-X is considering the future of life itself—
the ultimate goal, to live on other planets. Maezawa says,
I am small and always had a difficult time finding the right clothes.

His online clothing company made him a billionaire.
He bought Basquiat's Untitled (1982)—*a searing, talismanic
rendering of a skull*, according to Sotheby's—for $110 million.

The press release says he carries the hopes and dreams of all humankind,
but Maezawa knows there are things that can go wrong.
I'll have to train mentally so I'm not too worried up there.

*I don't like being alone. I have purchased every ticket.
I choose to go to the moon with artists!* Maezawa has not yet chosen
which film director, painter, novelist, musician, fashion designer,

sculptor, architect, photographer and dancer will go with him.
*When they see the moon up close, the curvature of the earth...
Just thinking about it now makes tears well up in my eyes.*

But concerning the cost of the tickets, Maezawa says,
*we've decided not to disclose that, at least for now.
My dream is not so much to go to space but to pursue world peace.*

MAY AS WELL PLAY

moondance as obscene as
          a bright head on the end of a billionaire
      who's sitting in the first spacecraft
        to take a vacation on the dark side
          knowing a few hundred only will follow
or, hey, tramping all over a long-standing symbol of the feminine spirit
though maybe not the cartoon state of originality one must have felt hitting
                golf balls there
but definitely the cost in lives and pain it took that patsy
           to plant his nation's night-black flag
        with all the self-awareness of a light bulb

SPACE

    i went out into cold, radiant darkness
        to where oceans dance unseen
    and you brush zones of recognition
        that will linger as enigma

    there the night is so immense it's like a face
    and there's that much sibilance inside the silence
it seems to be the start of the need to carve a garden
      from all one's wishes which quiver in stillness

    i drifted in eternity through gradations of madness
then at last found my place in an ancient perfect cadence

        now every evening i thank the nearest star
          that i was made to burn so fast
        that i was cursed with this great birth
          and that tomorrow never goes

MATT HETHERINGTON

EAGLE DEBRIEFING: STILL LIFE

When Armstrong backflipped
off the edge of the Earth,
his boot-prints were reproduced
in plaster-cast, in diminishing sizes,
to dance with the plaster ducks
down our loungeroom walls.

A wired-up Stars-and-Stripes was left behind
like the outstretched wing
of a taxidermied bird.
Or the sound of one hand's frantic clapping
in the moon's dead audience.

And afterwards (just as was feared),
the sports-vehicle recreationists came
to hoon all over the grey dune-scape—
then abandon their buggy up there
just parked any damned whichway
to the kerb of the Earth.

Mills & Boon burned their entire back-stock
of romances in the public square
and NASA got torched by lycanthropes,

as all the rest of us, meanwhile,
heaved and tossed in our sweaty beds—
feeling the moon's waning magic tingle
like an amputee's phantom pain.

SKYFALL

Things officially attested
as having fallen from the sky include:
wool thread, and candy,
winkles, worms, snakes,
frogs and toads,
varieties of beans and grains,
blood, meat, muscle and fat,
lizards, lichen, eels,
fish species of multifarious kinds
(catfish, trout, herring,
sardines, perch and suchlike) ...
Something described as 'angel hair'.
Glowing jelly, and green peaches,
flocks of birds—and banknotes.
Plus, a carpenter working on a roof
was impaled by a two-metre shaft of ice, one time.
There's meteors (or 'shooting stars'), of course,
and (too obvious to mention) Sun and Rain.
Then those usual suspects, the recalcitrant UFOs,
God—and Hope.

SKYFALL is derived from and extended from an original list in The Reader's Digest book *Mysteries of the Unknown*.

COMMUNION ELEMENTS

On the moon Buzz
Aldrin, Presbyterian,
asked for a moment's
peace to take a wafer, swill
some wine, body and blood of Jesus

Christ our Lord. Amen. Neil
Armstrong, Deist, determined
not to be a cunt,
watched the theatrics, letting
Buzz take the firsts

where he found them.
When Aldrin lurched off
with his workman's gait
to take man's first piss on the moon
Armstrong smelt wet ashes

and fireplace, and thought he heard
in the arc of earthlight
beyond cold silence
the resonant sound of *Adhan:*
the Muslim call to prayer.

CONSPIRACY THEORY

Laika, the space dog, did not die
from poisoned food
or disintegrate upon re-entry
but from overheating caused
by a malfunctioning thermal unit.

That was a secret for 45 years.

Laika, the space dog, possessing
smell 40 times greater than ours,
sensed post-humanly
the atmosphere's smaller
and smaller cage

before dying from overheating.

Laika the space dog, did not die,
but watches from orbit, expanding
to the size of an asteroid, a canine
umbilical dangling
into the upper atmosphere

like a lost foetus in Kubrick's *2001*.

CONSPIRACY

    'Buzz' Aldrin
      orbital king
        Doctor Rendezvous
      to friends
       projects long
      and perfect arc
    calculated
   actuated
with calmly milled
precision
  Maintains heading
   stays slide-rule true
    zero fear of ricochet
no chance of glancing
     off into space
Aged astronaut
still packs punch
  lands
  fist squarely
   on jabbering jaw
Blood inks doubter's
proffered Bible
  unsworn-upon
    by Second Man.

CLOSEST I'LL COME

Draining a long and hot bath
feels like re-entry. The whistling
departure of water screams
louder now, carries weightlessness
with it. Gravity locks on
to bring me in—me and my convex
capsule, off-white underbelly exposed,
shouldering our glowing way
through atmospheric fire.
Blackening reds, oranges, greens
and blues lick over
the open rim's ovoid edge,
fingering in
at my deep-slung safety.
Hopelessly heavy,
limbs pinned flat,
last litres sucking away,
I steer
my massive head up
in time to catch
the sudden undergills of three
bright mushrooms
lowering their naked Apollite
into the sea.

TOYSCAPE

a ball, yellow, blue
      soft when you touch it
hard when it hurtles through the air
      when you want to roll it on your skin
to take your pulse, temperature

splits apart, gathers around you
      like a pair of ear muffs
plays Bach on wind chimes
      multiplies so you can juggle
            split the space/time continuum
so you have more time

rockets at high speeds like an axe
      splits wood for the elderly
orbits the sun to trick astronomers
      lands in the sea and bounces on the surface
            to summon fish
make tsunamis for whaling ships

lands on the moon, bounces back
      to show NASA
            what a waste of time it is exploring
                space
circles Saturn, bounces back
      to show NASA what a waste
            of time it is
                exploring outer space

jumps into the chests of rocket scientists
      to help them go within

SEVEN MOON HAIKU

harbour light show—
a little boy points out
the half-moon

                                      2 a.m., full moon
                                      a badger scarpers
                                      for the shade

is the moon full?
he checks his app
97.8%

                                      halfway between
                                      moon and water
                                      moon's reflected light

romantic
moonlit walk, to check
the possum trap

                                      walking by the water
                                      moonlight
                                      follows

moonshadow puppets
a wolf chases a rabbit
to the camp fire

MOON

      Stripped
eye socket abyss
looks through. History
takes it as its sign. In
the garden its light is
rinsed in silence, its shadows
arcane, barbed. This
always opposite thing.
Mirror-like it admits
what is set before it,
divides dark water, wants
for nothing—
They walked onto its surface, would make it
small with flags—

SUN AND MOON

The lion loves the bone it breathes on
in the raked grass—

COUNTING BACKWARDS

1. BILDUNGSROMAN

America was stranger, more mysterious
than that old familiar face.
                          Nights following
we looked up at her peaches and cream
                                    blueing,
her pits and blemishes,
                        knowing she'd been trampled on
left bruised
            but still we chorused
                              'lift off!'
in borrowed voices
while the tide continued in and out,
                    rising and falling,
and our own inner seas began to form.

2. REIFUNGSROMAN

No-one I knew then had died.
I think of deep space now
                         as darkness,
how neither *infinite* nor *fathomless*
no word   quite suggests that stillness
broken now and then
                 by a shrug from the gods,
       a meteor shower,
stars which freckle a warm July sky,
     piercing the indigo border between us,
   scatterings of light that fall upon me
even as I look out into the unknown.

The critic Barbara Frey Waxman coined 'Reifungsroman' to suggest the concept of a story of ripening as women grow older.

O(R)BIT.

great sadness   we share the news   age of eighty-four
                Janet Shearon Armstrong lost

                    wife of test pilot   astronaut Neil Armstrong
    born   Wilmette, Illinois   youngest of three daughters
            School of Home Economics   Alpha Chi Omega sorority

    Jan and Neil married   eventually settled
San Gabriel mountains   outskirts   from their home

Jan could see her husband   flying   in the distance

                together, Jan and Neil   NASA space program
        and afterwards   after

38 years of marriage   Jan
                        and Neil divorced

everywhere she went, she forged   lifelong friendships
        Jan was founder and coach   supporter and advocate
founding member   Keep In Touch   group of
astronaut wives   remained close   survived
        sons   daughter-in-law, six grandchildren, two
great grandchildren   knew her   second child and
only daughter   died   brain tumour   two years, nine months
            many awards and honours
                                her courage
dedication during the American space program   all
remember   a strong, wilful woman

honour her by standing up
                        you believe

O(R)BIT. is an erasure poem using the obituary of Janet Shearon Armstong (1934 – 2018), published in the Houston Chronicle on June 27, 2018.

STABLE

Why be a workhorse when you could be a top-shelf
Arab mare singing country classics at daybreak,
galloping through traffic trailing stallions, perky
agents, blue ribbons and melting moments home-baked
in someone else's kitchen? We had a white one,
a twitchy coupé, everyone indulged her, and that works
for women too. Sometimes, some women, until it doesn't.
The trick is to be satisfied with the fruits of enchantment:
those fleshy clouds of fairy floss, big rocks
and box fresh shoes. Not always, though. There's also
the never-ending question, vertigo, the fist.
I like my stable, its earthen floor, fencepost heart
and clean chaff ready to go when I get back
from another day, willing to look wise in this halter.

.

FOR WHOM THE MOON: I

What is a moon, what is a mind,
what is a man, an area of darkness,
what is a mare, a getaway,
what is an astronaut, he carries out
instructions, obedient and armoured fœtus
whose woven and worn lunar tether
could be any hiker's failsafe terracotta
litter, if not returned to preserve with glass care
a memory few will ever have and some still say
didn't happen.
                    O tell us—
earth of breathable fabric, earth of eyes,
                    O tell us who we will not—
earth of spontaneous colour, earth of fools,
                    O tell us who we will not send,
unquenchable earth, to the moon…

FOR WHOM THE MOON: II

O tell us who we will and will not send,
discworld earth, to the moon,
                              to land
in the Sea of Tranquillity, to be saddled
with names from a science faulted with wonder,
as if there were seas on the moon, thirst
for seas that are states of mind, the sea of
Moscow also a state of mind?
                              Send
nobody who'll run mad across the sand,
no nightmare hippy wet behind the ears
looking for blooming moonflowers, burrowing
moonpups, moon roos boxing at the edge of
overly silver pools.
                              Send
the fair to middling housekeepers
who don't fix their clothes after they put them on
to go out, who are better at mending than ironing.
Kudos to the hoisters of flags with wrinkles,
showing the stars the stars, the overreached
symbol, the possible infinity
                              we can begin to count...

NEIL ARMSTRONG'S HEART

At liftoff the flight surgeon
clocked him at a brisk walk
the explosion that forced him
away from Earth the scale
of blast that blew three
predecessors to molecular bits
just a day at the office
to the prepared mind.

Touching down on the silver sea
Tranquility men had named it
so near to Fertility and Nectar
after alarms kept sounding
fuel enough for thirty seconds
and data overload on instruments
Armstrong's heart spiked as his foot
hit the silky powder raced so fast

there was no time between the first
and second stroke of its beats. So
the organism registers reality even
when the mind is trained to remain
stoic as a clock. He filled his pocket with rocks
set up seismometer and solar panels
to graph granular and angular shifts
left his outer boots on the moon

in case some form of life unrecognized
and unnamed had adhered to them
and might poison life on Earth
when they returned. After scrubdown
and quarantine the moonmen were safe again
to touch and be touched. Powder so fine
the surface feels like plaster, one said.
Another: I was going to say cement.

DEAR MOON

Spun off, kicked out, deflected space junk
little exile however you found your place
in our orbit how could we ever let you go
nameless up there in the black forever
pulling on our planet's seas and women's blood.

It was our men who made it first
envying our bodies' communion
with your magnetism. Thanks for the light
you borrowed and bounced back our way
apocalyptic fire turned by your regolith

into sheen and shapeliness, cosmetic glow—
all natural and free! No need to name a crater
Sea of Maybelline, Mare Estee Lauder.
Plato, Kepler, Copernicus, Apollo
even Jules Verne have cratered into the moon atlas.

What a conversation they must be having. Or is it
too cold up there to say a word? Maybe a little Venus
or Marie Curie would warm things up. Dear Moon,
science says you're drifting farther apart from us
but I promise you that art will never let you go.

FLY ME

1969

Which is the epic moment? Billowing-off or craft's fly-fall to
surface, huffing flames and dust, all those one

-eyed creatures in enormous skins fumbling down the ladder.
Still carried away a half-century later, they bounce and drift in
gorgeous clutziness, weight and its

-lessness in tense negotiation, stars backdropped against
the dark, oddly endearing. Who would know: inside the
suits they are slimmish, pink, almost hairless by mammalian
standards, too damned smooth. Do they realise how far out
there is until they think about getting back?

       So, space, what a joke, cold place
harbouring monsters, fire, a catch in the throat. Empty
-not empty, whatever they believe,

       they do the job: keep sprightly while the
camera runs, slightly comic in their dignity, boys cavorting
(The miracle: not only that they're up there, but through
space and time I can see them at it)

across the surface, trying to keep grounded. Now, they dance
to my command—hit play—grainy, black and white

(man, it looks like the moon or something),

their extreme high tech old-fashioned now, back

-sliding into the past.

2019

                I admit it: I too wanted to put my foot down,
who didn't? To play the game called Look at me, something to tell
the children I would never have, just as well

Given my mess of space. Blue eye looking askance. From here, I see
a grey face not looking back. If that lump of rock had a man in it,
he might wonder about us, might stop blowing his horns until I left
off gazing to consider

the world through his eyes, something closer to home. Please sir,
can you say cheese?

                Meanwhile, why do I love only from too far
away to reach? Why go anywhere at all, and also why not?

                Meanwhile, since I'm asking, who's driving this
spaceship, tell me who's reading the maps? Not I, joy

-riding through the void, fancy free, thought

-less, entirely without feck, concerned only with my street

-level destination, burning toward it, skidding right at the corner,
left at the second signal, speeding up. Orb in mind, what's the point
asking where or why, how or even whether we might ever come to
ground. Mean

-while, Happy birthday Lander, you who put down. Happy
birthday, Moon, put upon. For us, oh Earth, idea, touchstone,
vehicle on which time sorts us: help us, won't you, hold together
here?

EAGLE AT TRANQUILITY

I wasn't the first one to get here, but I am the last to leave. *Report*, says a voice on the radio, and I reply: *Baby, things are going just swimmingly.*

Daily I do the things that astronauts do: collect rocks; plant flags. My daughter watches through her binoculars, and I wave, in case she can see. She is making a scrapbook of my life. Every day she tunes in to the radio, learning about sound and the way it moves—like water; like light.

You're looking good in every respect, says the radio, and I am. There's a flag suspended above a footprint. Something's upside down: a suspense of light. There's a weather station: rain gauge propped against rock, solar panel running amuck. Readings are off the scale.

My daughter has built a weather station in her bedroom and is recording shivers of sound. I shout her name, in case she can hear.

A voice on the radio says *stand b*y, and I do. Drifting through gravity beside the mast I adjust each day, my spirit level recording miniscule shifts. Waiting to hear *you are confirmed go for orbit.* Waiting to go.

Partly redacted from John Noble Wilford, 'Astronauts land on plain; collect rocks, plant flag', New York Times, July 21, 1969; and from Apollo 11 Spacelog transcript, Tape 1/3, Page 3.

ON THE DARKER SIDE

You are in the back room polishing glass that's inches thick and if you've done the maths right you will have ground yourself a lens, concavities and depth perfectly aligned. But $(n-1)(1/R1-1/R2)$ does not always equal $1/f$, or maybe you got the numbers wrong, and anyway you watch a crack bleed across the glass. *That's thermal shock*, says old George from the Men's Shed, who knows his stuff. *What you need is*—and he pushes you aside—*do it like this*, firm and steady, bring the glass to the wheel.

When you look through the lens he's crafted
        the sky shatters
                a kaleidoscope
                        all wild distortion

You think you'll stay. Pull up a chair, watch the stars roll past on their slippery-slope run to somewhere. Try fishing with that sinker made of snow, a hook drawn from your eye. When you cast the line you catch the moon.

BIOGRAPHIES

CASSANDRA ATHERTON is an award-winning writer and scholar of prose poetry. She was a Visiting Scholar in English at Harvard University and a Visiting Fellow in Literature at Sophia University, Tokyo. She has published 17 critical and creative books. Her most recent books of prose poetry are *PreRaphaelite* (2018) and *Touch* (forthcoming).

CHRISTIAN BÖK is the author of *Eunoia* (2001), a bestselling work of experimental literature, which has gone on to win the Griffin Prize for Poetic Excellence. Bök is a Fellow of the Royal Society of Canada, and he teaches at Charles Darwin University.

ROBYN BOLAM's latest Bloodaxe collection is *Hyem* (October 2017). Her selected poems, *New Wings* (2007), was a Poetry Book Society Recommendation. She also compiled *Eliza's Babes: four centuries of women's poetry in English* (Bloodaxe, 2005) and was Hampshire Poet 2018. www.robynbolam.com

LISA BROCKWELL lives on a rural property near Byron Bay. Her poems have been published in *The Spectator*, *The Canberra Times*, *The Weekend Australian*, *Meanjin* and *Best Australian Poems*. Her first collection, *Earth Girls*, was published by Pitt Street Poetry in 2016 and commended in the Anne Elder Award.

OWEN BULLOCK has published three collections of poetry: *sometimes the sky isn't big enough* (Steele Roberts, 2010), *semi* (Puncher & Wattmann, 2017) and *Work & Play* (Recent Work Press, 2017); four books of haiku, and a novella. Owen has a PhD in Creative Writing from the University of Canberra, where he currently teaches. poetry-in-process.com

MAGGIE BUTT was a journalist and BBC TV documentary producer turned poet and novelist. Her collections include: *Lipstick*, *Ally Pally Prison Camp* and *Degrees of Twilight*. She has taught at Middlesex University, London since 1990 and is a Royal Literary Fund Advisory Fellow. www.maggiebutt.co.uk

ANNE CALDWELL is a poet and lecturer for the Open University. She is also a PhD student at the University of Bolton. Her latest poetry collection is *Painting the Spiral Staircase*, Cinnamon, 2016.

VAHNI CAPILDEO is a Trinidadian Scottish writer whose books include the experimental theatre of *Skin Can Hold*, completed during a Douglas Caster Cultural Fellowship at the University of Leeds, and *Measures of Expatriation* (Forward Poetry Prizes Best Collection award, 2016).

ANNE CASEY is author of two poetry collections and was a journalist, magazine editor, media communications director and legal author for 25+ years,. Her work is widely published internationally and ranks in *The Irish Times* 'Most-Read'. She is Senior Poetry Editor of *Other Terrain* and *Backstory* journals (Swinburne University, Melbourne).

EILEEN CHONG is the author of eight books, most recently *Rainforest* from Pitt Street Poetry, and *Dark Matter* from Recent Work Press. Her work has shortlisted for several awards, including twice for the Prime Minister's Literary Awards. She lives and works in Sydney, Australia. www.eileenchong.com.au

PAUL CLIFF is a Canberra writer and editor. His collection, *A Constellation of Abnormalities* (Puncher & Wattmann, 2017) won the ACT Writers Centre Award for Poetry. His collection of poems on Canberra and region was published in 2019.

KATHARINE COLES' seventh collection of poems *Wayward*, was published in June 2019; her memoir, *Look Both Ways*, was released in 2018. Coles has received grants and fellowships from the NEA, the NEH, the NSF, and the Guggenheim Foundation. She is a Distinguished Professor at the University of Utah.

OLIVER COMINS lives and works in West London. He is old enough to have been following aspects of the "space race" in the 1960s. Templar Poetry published a full-length collection *Oak Fish Island* in 2018.

TRICIA DEARBORN is an award-winning poet whose work has been widely published in Australian literary journals, as well as in the UK, the US, Ireland, New Zealand and online. Dearborn's previous collections are *The Ringing World* and *Frankenstein's Bathtub*. Her third poetry collection, *Autobiochemistry*, is available from UWA Publishing.

BENJAMIN DODDS is a Sydney poet who was raised in the Riverina. His debut collection is *Regulator* (Puncher & Wattmann, 2014). Dodds's work has appeared in *Best Australian Poems 2014*, *Meanjin*, *Southerly* and on RN's *Poetica* and *Science Friction* programs. He co-judged the *Quantum Words Science Poetry Competition* in 2018.

MARTIN DOLAN is a Canberra-based poet. His second collection, *Peripheral Vision*, was published in 2018. Martin is a PhD candidate in creative writing at the University of Canberra. He is also working on a new collection, due for release in 2020.

ROSS DONLON's books *include The Blue Dressing Gown, Sjovegen—The Sea Road—50 tanka for Alvik* and *Lucidity*. He has featured at poetry festivals and other readings both in Australia and Europe.

MAURA DOOLEY's most recent collections are *The Silvering* (Bloodaxe) and *Negative of a Group Photograph* (Bloodaxe) (with Elhum Shakerifa) of work by the exiled Iranian poet Azita Ghahreman. She teaches at Goldsmiths, University of London and is a Fellow of the Royal Society of Literature.

MOIRA EGAN's most recent books are *Synæsthesium* (The New Criterion Prize, 2017) and *Olfactorium* (Italic PesQuod, 2018). She lives in Rome, Italy and teaches Creative Writing at St. Stephen's School.

NILOOFAR FANAIYAN is a writer and poet who has lived in the US, Australia, the Netherlands, Tanzania and Israel. She was the 2016 Donald Horne Research Fellow at the Centre for Creative and Cultural Research, University of Canberra, where she obtained her PhD. She received the Canberra Critics Circle Literary Award for Poetry for her first book of poems titled *Transit* (RWP, 2016).

D.W. FENZA served for two decades as the executive director of an American association of writers and creative writing programs. He is the author of a book-length poem, *The Interlude*.

JOHN FOULCHER's twelfth book of poetry, *Dancing with Stephen Hawking*, will be published by Pitt Street Poetry in 2020. He lives in Canberra. He has always been a science fiction fan, even when it's not fiction.

LISA GORTON is a poet, novelist and essayist. She lives in Melbourne. Her two most recent works, both from Giramondo, are the poetry collection *Empirical* (2019) and a novel, *The Life of Houses*.

SAMIA GOUDIE is a Bundjalung Aboriginal Australian woman. Selections of her poetry have appeared in publications such as *Southerly, IWR International writers online, Indigenous poetry journal*, and *Too deadly, our voice, our way our business* by Us Mob Writers. She is Associate Professor in the School of Arts and design at the University of Canberra.

PHILIP GROSS has published some twenty collections of poetry, winning the T.S. Eliot Prize 2009. He is a keen collaborator with artists, musicians and writers, most recently with Lesley Saunders on *A Part of the Main*, and with scientists on *Dark Sky Park*, a collection for young people (both 2018.)

OZ HARDWICK is a writer, photographer and occasional musician, based in York (UK). He has published eight poetry collections, most recently *The Lithium Codex* (Hedgehog, 2019), and has edited and co-edited several more, including (with Miles Salter) *The Valley Press Anthology of Yorkshire Poetry*, which was a UK National Poetry Day recommendation in 2017. Oz is Professor of English at Leeds Trinity University, where he leads the Creative Writing programmes. www.ozhardwick.co.uk

ALISON HAWTHORNE DEMING's most recent books are the poetry collection *Stairway to Heaven* (Penguin 2016), and the essay collection *Zoologies: On Animals and the Human Spirit* (Milkweed 2014). She is Agnese Nelms Haury Chair in Environment and Social Justice and Regents' Professor at the University of Arizona.

DOMINIQUE HECQ grew up in the French-speaking part of Belgium. She now lives in Melbourne. Her works include a novel, three collections of short stories and eight books of poetry. Often experimental, her writing explores love, loss, exile, and the possibilities of language. *After Cage* (2019) is her most recent collection. She is a recipient of the 2018 International Best Poets Prize, IPTRC.

MATT HETHERINGTON is a writer, music-maker, teacher, and part-time DJ. He is also on the board of the Australian Haiku Society. Some current inspirations are: Denise Levertov, Wollumbin seen from a distance, and Vietnamese mint. matthetherington.net

PAUL HETHERINGTON's most recent poetry collections are *Palace of Memory: An Elegy* (RWP, 2019) and *Moonlight on Oleander: Prose Poems* (UWAP, 2018). He has won or been shortlisted for numerous national and international awards and is Professor of Writing in the Faculty of Arts and Design at the University of Canberra. He is head of the International Poetry Studies Institute (IPSI) and founded the International Prose Poetry Group in 2014.

ANDY JACKSON has featured as a poet and a performer at literary events and arts festivals in Ireland, India, the US and Australia. His most recent collection, *Music our bodies can't hold* (Hunter Publishers, 2017), consists of portrait poems of other people with Marfan Syndrome.

JILL JONES' most recent books are *Viva the Real, Brink, Breaking the Days,* shortlisted for the 2017 Kenneth Slessor Prize, and *The Beautiful Anxiety,* which won the 2015 Victorian Premiers' Literary Award for Poetry. Her work features in recent anthologies including *Contemporary Australian Poetry* and *Contemporary Australian Feminist Poetry.*

BELLA LI is the author of *Argosy* (Vagabond Press, 2017), which won the 2018 Victorian Premier's Literary Award for Poetry and the 2018 NSW Premier's Literary Award for Poetry. Her most recent book, *Lost Lake* (Vagabond Press, 2018), was shortlisted for the 2018 QLD Literary Award for Poetry.

IAN MCMILLAN is a writer and radio presenter who makes poems, song lyrics and plays and who loves collaborating with musicians and visual artists to create pieces that are bigger than the sum of their parts.

PAUL MILLS was recently an RLF Fellow at the University of York. He is working on a new collection of poems exploring human prehistory and early civilisations. Previous books were published by Carcanet Press and Smith Doorstop, with pamphlets from Wayleave Press and Smith Doorstop. paulmillswrtiting.co.uk

PAUL MUNDEN is a poet, editor and screenwriter living in North Yorkshire. He is an Adjunct Associate Professor at the University of Canberra and a Royal Literary Fund Fellow at the University of Leeds. The inaugural director of the *Poetry on the Move* poetry festival (2015-2017), he has published five collections, most recently *Chromatic* (UWA Publishing, 2017).

HELEN MORT lives in Sheffield, England. She has published two collections with Chatto & Windus, *Division Street* and *No Map Could Show Them.* Her work has been shortlisted for the Costa Prize and the T.S. Eliot Prize.

NESSA O'MAHONY is an Irish poet who has published five books of poetry, the most recent being *The Hollow Woman on the Island* (Salmon Poetry 2019). She also writes crime fiction.

MARIO PETRUCCI is an award-winning poet, ecologist and PhD physicist who has held major poetry residencies at the Imperial War Museum and with BBC Radio 3. *Heavy Water: a poem for Chernobyl* (Enitharmon, 2004) secured the Daily Telegraph/ Arvon Prize. *i tulips* (Enitharmon, 2010) exemplifies Petrucci's distinctive combination of innovation and humanity. www.mariopetrucci.com

GEOFF PAGE is based in Canberra. He has published twenty-three collections of poetry as well as two novels, five verse novels and several other works. Among his awards is the ACU Poetry Prize for 2017. His latest books include *Hard Horizons* (Pitt Street Poetry, 2017) and *Elegy for Emily* (Puncher & Wattmann, 2019).

ALVIN PANG is a poet and editor based in Singapore. Featured in the *Oxford Companion to Modern Poetry in English*, and the *Penguin Book of the Prose Poem*, he has been published internationally in more than twenty languages, including Swedish and Croatian. His latest book is *WHAT HAPPENED: Poems 1997-2017*.

RENEÉ PETTITT-SCHIPP is an award-winning writer and educator. Renee's work with asylum seekers in detention on Christmas Island inspired her first collection of poetry *The Sky Runs Right Through Us* released by UWA Publishing in 2018. Reneé now lives in Western Australia's deep south.

LUCY SHEERMAN runs the University of Cambridge Centre for Creative Writing. She is currently working on a series of essays and fan fictions which respond to *Jane Eyre*. Publications include: *Rarefied* (Oystercatcher), *Fragments Salvaged from her Diary* (Dancing Girl Press), *Even You Song* (First Hand Records) and *Pine Island* (Cam Rivers).

ALEX SKOVRON is the author of six poetry collections, a prose novella and a book of short stories, *The Man who Took to his Bed* (2017). His latest volume of poetry, *Towards the Equator: New & Selected Poems* (2014), was shortlisted in the Prime Minister's Literary Awards. He lives in Melbourne.

MELINDA SMITH has published six books of poetry, most recently *Goodbye, Cruel* (Pitt St Poetry, 2017). She won the 2014 Prime Minister's Literary Award for *Drag down to unlock or place an emergency call*. She is based in the ACT and is a former poetry editor of the *Canberra Times*.

SHANE STRANGE's writing has appeared in various print and on-line journals in Australia, the US, and the UK. He is publisher at Recent Work Press, and is Director of the *Poetry on the Move* festival, 2018-19.

KEIJIRO SUGA (b. 1958) is a Japanese poet and critic based in Tokyo. He has published five collections of poetry in Japanese and his chapbook in English, *Transit Blues*, was published in 2018 by IPSI (The International Poetry Studies Institute). This has been translated in Spanish and published in Spain in 2019.

JAMES SUTHERLAND SMITH was born in 1948 and lives in Slovakia. He is retired university lecturer in Cultural Studies and has published seven collections of his own poetry besides translating a number of Slovak and Serbian poets into English. For his translations he received the Slovak Hviezdoslav Prize in 2003 and the Serbian Zlatko Krasni Prize in 2014.

JEN WEBB is Director of the Centre for Creative and Cultural Research. Recent publications include *Researching Creative Writing* (Frontinus, 2015), and the poetry collection *Moving Targets* (Recent Work Press, 2018).

RIVER WOLTON is a former Derbyshire Poet Laureate whose collections include *Leap* and *Indoor Skydiving*. A writing facilitator with schools, community groups and people of all ages, she recently held a short residency in an 18th century lead mine.

2019 Editions
Palace of Memory: An elegy **Paul Hetherington**
Acting Like a Girl **Sandra Renew**
A Coat of Ashes **Jackson**
Summer Haiku **Owen Bullock**
A Common Garment **Anita Patel**
Giant Steps: Reflections on Apollo 11 and beyond **Various**
Some Sketchy Notes on Matter **Angela Gardner**
Canberra Light **Paul Cliff**
A Wardrobe of Selves **Peter Bakowski**
Breathing in Stormy Seasons **Stephanie Green**
Strange Creatures **Alyson Miller**

2018 Editions
The Uncommon Feast **Eileen Chong**
Inlandia **KA Nelson**
Peripheral Vision **Martin Dolan**
The Love of the Sun **Matt Hetherington**
Moving Targets **Jen Webb**
Things I Have Thought to Tell You Since I Saw You Last **Penelope Layland**
The Many Uses of Mint **Ravi Shankar**
Abstractions **Various**
ACE: Arresting,Contemporary stories by Emerging Writers **Various**

all titles available from
www.recentworkpress.com

www.ingramcontent.com/pod-product-compliance
Lightning Source LLC
Chambersburg PA
CBHW032043290426
44110CB00012B/936